D1713216

THE MOST INFLUENTIAL
WOMEN
IN STEM

BREAKING THE GLASS CEILING
THE MOST INFLUENTIAL WOMEN™

THE MOST INFLUENTIAL
WOMEN
IN STEM

Barbara Allman

Rosen
YA
New York

To Suzi and Carol, my remarkable sisters

Published in 2019 by The Rosen Publishing Group, Inc.
29 East 21st Street, New York, NY 10010

First Edition

Library of Congress Cataloging-in-Publication Data

Names: Allman, Barbara, author.
Title: The most influential women in STEM / Barbara Allman.
Description: New York : Rosen Publishing, 2019. | Series: Breaking the glass ceiling: the most influential women | Includes bibliographical references and index. | Audience: Grades 7–12.
Identifiers: LCCN 2017055427| ISBN 9781508179696 (library bound) | ISBN 9781508179849 (pbk.)
Subjects: LCSH: Women in science—History—Juvenile literature. | Women scientists—Biography—Juvenile literature.
Classification: LCC Q130 .A48625 2019 | DDC 509.2/52—dc23
LC record available at https://lccn.loc.gov/2017055427

Manufactured in the United States of America

On the cover: Sally Ride made history on June 18, 1984, when she became the first American woman to go to space. She later investigated shuttle crashes for NASA and taught university-level physics.

CONTENTS

INTRODUCTION

For millennia, people have wondered about the natural world and worked to unravel its mysteries. Until the twentieth century, most women did not have access to the education or tools necessary to do scientific work. In fact, very few people had those options, and those who did were usually educated elite men. The profiles in this book highlight the creative, determined, and insightful women across the centuries and around the world who followed their intellectual curiosity and overcame substantial barriers to enter the world of STEM: science, technology, engineering, and mathematics.

Well into the twentieth century, women were discouraged from studying the hard sciences, and those who wanted to do so had few role models. The women who made their marks in STEM have opened doors and minds for others to do the same. Many of these women have received the highest accolades in their fields, including the Nobel Prizes for Chemistry, Physics, and Physiology or Medicine; MacArthur Fellowships; and the Fields Medal for mathematics. Several were the first women to earn these awards and to reach the summit of their professions.

Many of these women encountered discrimination based not only on gender, but also on class, religion, and ethnicity. Women from ancient Greece to nineteenth-

Tu Youyou is presented with the 2015 Nobel Prize in Physiology or Medicine by King Carl XVI Gustaf of Sweden. Tu's malaria therapy was hailed as "of immeasurable benefit to mankind."

century America were largely barred from the study and practice of medicine because of their gender. Yet Elizabeth Blackwell, Alice Ball, and Virginia Apgar made major contributions to medical science. People of the lower classes were excluded from the emerging science of geology. Yet self-educated, nineteenth-century working-class woman Mary Anning discovered, identified, and classified hundreds of fossils, contributing to the foundations of paleontology. Women were assumed to be incapable of scientific thought. Yet Barbara McClintock's theory of genetic transposition, or "jumping genes," was central to the development of genetics and earned her a Nobel Prize many years later. The rise of Nazism and Fascism forced many European Jewish scientists into hiding. Yet despite this persecution, Rita Levi-Montalcini set up a lab to conduct research that later provided the mechanism to combat diseases of the nervous system. Minorities have systematically been excluded from pursuing careers in STEM. Yet there are black engineers, Asian chemists, Hispanic astronauts, Middle Eastern mathematicians, and Native American physicians.

The story of STEM is the story not only of accomplished men, but also of exceptional women, minorities, people of varying classes, ethnicities, and religions. Meet some of the most influential women in STEM.

CHAPTER ONE

WOMEN IN MEDICINE

Women have typically been responsible for managing the home and family, attending to the physical health of their family members, drawing from their own experiences and from information passed on from one generation to another. Until the 1900s, few women were able to pursue medical science as a profession. Certain remarkable women persisted in their efforts to become formally trained doctors. Some even established their own women-only institutions to do so. A particular interest in improving the health of women and children has helped women to make important strides in that area of the medical field.

Merit Ptah (c. 2700 BCE): Chief Physician in Ancient Egypt

Unlike in most other societies, ancient or modern, women in ancient Egypt were equal to men and had the same rights. They were entitled to own businesses and land, to divorce their spouses, to practice medicine, and to rule the country. There were

Reliefs honoring important women, such as this unidentified goddess, are found carved on Egyptian royal tombs. An image of Merit Ptah, chief physician, was found near the pyramid at Saqqara.

women physicians and midwives, as well as all-women medical schools.

Merit Ptah, who lived in Egypt around 2700 BCE, was chief physician of the pharaoh's court. As chief physician, it is likely that she taught and supervised other physicians in addition to attending to the pharaoh, although it is not known which pharaoh she served. Merit Ptah is believed to be the first female physician in history to be mentioned by name. Her name means "beloved of the god Ptah." Her image is carved on the limestone wall of a tomb near Egypt's oldest pyramid, the step pyramid at Saqqara, along with the inscription "the Chief Physician," which was arranged by her son, a high priest. A crater on the planet Venus is named for Merit Ptah.

AGNODICE BEATS THE SYSTEM

In a collection titled *Fabulae*, Roman writer Gaius Julius Hyginus told the story of Agnodice, a fourth-century Athenian woman physician and midwife who specialized in medicine for women, particularly those giving birth. Because women were not allowed to study medicine in Athens at that time, Agnodice is said to have cut her hair and disguised herself as a man in order to train and then to practice medicine.

(continued on the next page)

(continued from the previous page)

She became sought after by women in labor who refused treatment from male physicians. As her popularity grew, she was viewed as a threat by male physicians, who accused her of corruption. Agnodice was put on trial. During the trial, she revealed her identity as a woman. She was then accused of practicing medicine as a woman, which was illegal. Wives of the prominent men of Athens came to her defense, insisting that her treatments were effective. Agnodice was set free, and the law forbidding female physicians was repealed.

Scholars debate the historical existence of Agnodice because of inconsistencies in the dates she was purported to have lived and studied, and the claim that there were no female midwives in Athens before her. However, she has been referred to since the sixteenth century as setting a precedent for women to practice medicine.

Dr. Elizabeth Blackwell (1821–1910): British American Physician

Born in England in 1821, Elizabeth Blackwell was the third of nine children. Her father, Samuel Blackwell, believed that each of his children should receive an education. As a result, Blackwell and her siblings were highly educated and intellectually stimulated. The family emigrated to the United States in 1832.

Driven by financial need, Blackwell and two sisters started a school for young women, and then Blackwell took a series of teaching positions. When a friend dying of cancer told Blackwell her ordeal would have been better if she had been cared for by a female doctor, Blackwell was inspired to pursue a career in medicine.

Despite the support of two physicians with whom she boarded while teaching, Blackwell was rejected by a series of medical schools. She was admitted to Geneva Medical College in upstate New York in 1847, after all 150 male students at the school voted to admit her. Some accounts say her acceptance was meant to be a joke. Regardless, Blackwell made the most of her opportunity.

Blackwell faced many challenges during her time there. She was forced to sit separately to attend lectures, and she was derided as a "bad" woman by the people of the town. However, Blackwell ultimately earned the respect of her classmates and professors, and in 1849 graduated first in her class, becoming the first woman to earn a medical degree in the United States.

Blackwell continued her training in London and Paris, where she was consigned to nursing or midwifery. She came to recognize that personal hygiene and preventative care were crucial to preventing the spread of disease. Returning to the

72   FRANK LESLIE'S ILLUSTRATED NEWSPAPER.   [APRIL 16, 1870.

NEW YORK CITY.—MEDICAL COLLEGE FOR WOMEN, EAST TWELFTH STREET AND SECOND AVENUE—THE ANATOMICAL LECTURE-ROOM.—SEE PAGE 71.

In this print from 1870, female medical students attend an anatomy lecture at the Women's Medical College, which was established by Elizabeth Blackwell in New York City.

United States in 1851, Blackwell faced prejudice as a female doctor and found it difficult to acquire patients or to secure positions in hospitals. In the mid-1850s, she opened a small clinic for poor women and children. And in 1857, she and her sister Emily Blackwell, a surgeon and the third woman to earn a medical degree in the United States, founded the New York Infirmary for Indigent Women and Children.

A primary goal of the institute was to provide jobs for women physicians.

Blackwell opened the Women's Medical College of the New York Infirmary in 1868, and after a year returned to England. In 1874, she joined other pioneering physicians Sophia Jex-Blake, Emily Blackwell, Elizabeth Garrett Anderson, and Thomas Henry to establish the London School of Medicine for Women, where she taught gynecology. In 1877, the Royal Free Hospital became the first hospital to allow women from the medical school to work and complete their clinical studies. The school's early graduates included the first female doctor in South Africa, the first female obstetrician from India, and the first British female pharmacist. Today, the London School of Medicine for Women is merged with the University College Hospital Medical School.

The title of Blackwell's autobiography best describes her legacy: *Pioneer Work in Opening the Medical Profession to Women*. Her vision and her work laid the groundwork for many women to gain access to medical training and jobs as physicians.

Alice Ball (1892–1916): African American Chemist

Alice Ball was born in 1892 and, except for a year spent in Hawaii, grew up in Washington State. From an educated, well-off family, Ball excelled in science in high school. She earned two undergraduate degrees,

This image of the Kalaupapa Leper Colony on Molokai was probably taken during the early twentieth century. Today, the United States National Park Service preserves the historic buildings that remain.

one in pharmaceutical chemistry and one in pharmacy, from the University of Washington. Ball and her professor of pharmacy published an article in the *Journal of the American Chemical Society*, after which Ball received several scholarship offers to continue her studies. She opted to return to Hawaii, accepting an offer from the College of Hawaii. There, she focused on the chemical properties of chaulmoogra oil, which had been used with moderate success to treat leprosy.

Ball earned her master's degree in 1915, becoming the first woman and the first African American to earn a graduate degree from the College of Hawaii (now the University of Hawaii). She went on to become the first woman and African American chemistry professor at the university. She continued her study of chaulmoogra oil.

Leprosy, also known as Hansen's disease, is an infection with no initial symptoms. Untreated, it eventually causes nerve damage, preventing a person from feeling pain. People with leprosy may lose parts of their hands and feet because of repeated injuries or infections they simply cannot feel. Leprosy is contagious and for thousands of years was considered extremely dangerous. People suffering from leprosy were banished to isolated places. In Hawaii, they were permanently quarantined on the island of Molokai.

It was known that oil from the seeds of the chaulmoogra tree was effective in treating leprosy, but it was thick, sticky, and had an acrid flavor, so it was difficult to administer topically, by injection, or orally. At the age of twenty-three, Ball created a water-soluble chemical compound from chaulmoogra oil that could be injected, making it the only effective treatment for leprosy.

Ball died in 1916, at the age of twenty-four. It is thought that she accidentally inhaled chlorine gas in a lab class she was teaching at the college and it damaged her lungs. She died before she could publish her findings, which would have established the work as hers. The president of the university continued Ball's work, producing large quantities of the injectable chaulmoogra extract, and taking credit for Ball's findings and the full recovery of seventy-eight patients. It wasn't until 2000 that Ball was given credit for her work and was honored by the University of Hawaii with its Board of Regents Medal of Distinction and a plaque.

Thanks to Ball's work, people with leprosy were no longer forced to live in quarantine. More than eight thousand people were able to be treated at home, and with consistently successful results. The chaulmoogra extract was the preferred treatment for leprosy until the 1940s.

Dr. Virginia Apgar (1909–1974): American Obstetrical Anesthesiologist

Virginia Apgar liked to quip that her family "never sat down." Despite this, one brother was chronically ill as a child, and the other died of tuberculosis. These events sparked Apgar's interest in becoming a doctor. Born and raised in Westfield, New Jersey, Apgar studied zoology at Mount Holyoke College, graduating in 1929. Highly energetic, she pursued many interests as a student, including writing for the school newspaper, participating in several sports, and playing violin and cello in the school's orchestra. Throughout her life, Apgar maintained her interest in the violin, as well as in gardening, fly-fishing, stamp collecting, golfing, and, later, flying.

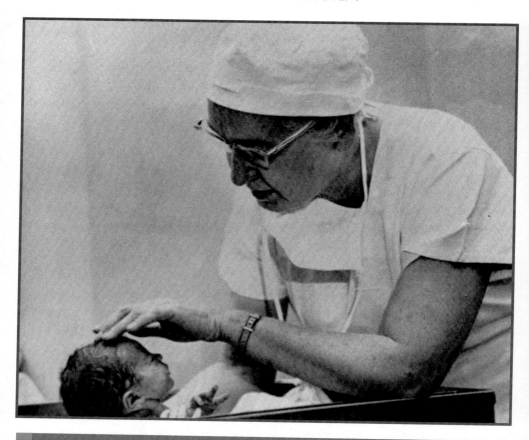

Virginia Apgar closely assesses the health of a newborn baby in her care. The Apgar scoring method is used at one minute and five minutes after birth.

Apgar earned her medical degree from Columbia University of Physicians and Surgeons, and, separately, acquired a certification in anesthesiology. She returned to the university as director of anesthesiology and became the first female professor there. Apgar is best known for developing the Apgar score, a system used to determine the health of newborn babies in the first few minutes of life. Her innovative point system gave doctors an organized method for assessing newborns by measuring heart rate, respiratory effort, muscle tone, skin coloring, and reflexive response immediately after birth. Points are given for each observation and then totaled to determine if the baby needs emergency care.

Apgar also pioneered the use of an alternative anesthesia when she and two colleagues determined that cyclopropane, the type most commonly administered to mothers giving birth, was detrimental to their infants and often resulted in low Apgar scores. The research papers Apgar published on the subject convinced other physicians to change their choice of anesthesia.

Later in her career, Apgar focused on parent education with her 1972 book, *Is My Baby All Right?*, along with many articles in magazines and newspapers. She made TV appearances and became well known to the general public for her work toward the prevention of birth defects and later as a director of what is now the March of Dimes.

Dr. Tu Youyou (1930–): Chinese Chemist, Nobel Prize Winner

Tu Youyou was born in Ningbo, China, in 1930. Her family valued education and ensured that Tu and her four brothers attended top schools. When she was sixteen, Tu contracted tuberculosis, which kept her out of school for two years. During this time, she decided on a career in medical research to keep herself and others healthy.

Tu earned her medical degree in 1955 at Beijing Medical College and then attended the Academy of Traditional Chinese Medicine. Her dual training in modern and traditional medicine played a key role in her later research. In 1969, Tu was assigned to lead a team of researchers tasked with finding a cure for malaria using Chinese traditional medicines. This was during the Cultural Revolution, a period when China's communist leader Mao Zedong imposed complete control over the Chinese government and people. Many leaders and experts who were considered insufficiently supportive of the government were prevented from carrying out their work, so the government turned to less experienced people. As a young scientist, Tu was both motivated and overwhelmed by the pressure to perform this all-encompassing and important work, which was done at great personal cost. She placed her two young daughters in the care of others while she conducted her research. Neither recognized Tu when she was finally able to bring them home several years later.

Malaria is a deadly disease caused by a parasite carried by mosquitoes. It killed hundreds of thousands of people each year. Tu and her research team interviewed experienced Chinese medical practitioners and pored over traditional Chinese medical literature to collect more than two thousand recipes. Tu narrowed this down to 640 prescriptions containing plants that were said to have some effectiveness in fighting malaria. She and her team tested 380 extracts from 200 herbs, finally isolating the effective compound—what Tu named *qinghaosu,* or artemisinin—in a plant called sweet wormwood, or *qinghao.* Tu realized that the standard method of extracting artemisinin, boiling the plant in water, actually damaged the important property. Instead, she used low temperatures to extract the artemisinin, testing the extraction first on mice and monkeys, and then on herself. Many clinical trials confirmed the effectiveness of the drug, and artemisinin-based drug therapy is now the recommended treatment for malaria.

Tu's knowledge of Western medicine and traditional Chinese herbal medicine led her team to find a cure for malaria that saved millions of lives around the world, particularly in Asia and Africa. She was unable to publish the results of her team's work because of governmental restrictions on the publication of scientific information, but they released their findings anonymously in 1977. However, by the early 1980s, Tu's work had reached the international community, and in 2000, the World Health Organization (WHO) recommended a combination of artemisinin and other drugs as the first-line treatment for malaria. Tu has received numerous awards for her work. She is one of three medical researchers to receive the 2015 Nobel Prize for Physiology or Medicine.

Lori Arviso Alvord holds her autobiography, *The Scalpel and the Silver Bear*. It tells of her experiences using both modern Western and traditional Native American medicine to heal.

Dr. Lori Arviso Alvord (1958–): Navajo Surgeon

Dr. Lori Arviso Alvord grew up on a Navajo reservation in the small New Mexico town of Crownpoint. Half Navajo and half white, Alvord earned good grades in high school and was determined to get a college degree. When she learned that Dartmouth College had a small but supportive group of Native American students, she applied there and was accepted at age sixteen. Among one of the first women and one of few Native Americans to attend Dartmouth, she faced sexism and racism on campus. She keenly felt the cultural differences between Indian and non-Indian students. She disliked the highly competitive environment she found at the Ivy League school and sought *hozho*, which means "walking in beauty," and describes a Navajo lifestyle of balance and harmony. Alvord graduated in 1979 with a double major in psychology and sociology.

Alvord took a job in medical research with Dr. Gary Rosenberg at the University of New Mexico. Rosenberg encouraged her to take premed classes, where she found parallels between science and traditional Navajo teachings. She went on to train as a surgeon at Stanford University Medical School, and she became the first female Diné (Navajo) board-certified surgeon.

Alvord returned to her Navajo reservation to serve the community. She soon discovered that although she had technical proficiency as a surgeon, she was not yet a healer capable of curing the whole patient. In the tradition of her people, everything is connected, and sickness occurs when something is out of balance. Healing is about restoring balance and harmony and treating the whole person—body, spirit, environment, and relationships. Early in her practice, Alvord incorporated culture-specific behaviors into her work, such as touching her patients with respect and only when necessary, not rushing their responses to her questions, and gaining their trust. She treated her patients like family.

Alvord believes that psychological and spiritual methods, as well as physical, are important for helping her patients to heal. Patients who feel understood and cared for fare better. She establishes a calm and serene atmosphere in her operating room and envisions beautifying old hospitals so they become healing environments. In her book, *The Scalpel and the Silver Bear*, she describes the experiences that led her to develop her approach to medical caregiving in hopes of changing the nation's health care delivery system. Alvord has served on the faculties of several colleges, including Dartmouth's. She was nominated for surgeon general of the United States in 2013.

CHAPTER TWO

WOMEN IN BIOLOGY AND EARTH SCIENCE

Some of the most stunning discoveries in the fields of biology and earth science have been made by women. At a time when scientists thought worms and insects could spontaneously generate from mud or cheese, a woman naturalist and illustrator looked closer and chronicled a caterpillar's metamorphosis with her artist's eye. A girl taught herself animal anatomy to analyze, classify, and describe the fossils she chiseled from the cliffs near her home. A female geneticist proved that genes move instead of remaining fixed to chromosomes. And a female biologist sparked the environmental movement by documenting the deleterious effects of pesticides.

Maria Sibylla Merian (1647–1717): German Naturalist and Illustrator

Maria Sibylla Merian was born in Frankfurt, Germany. Her father was an engraver and publisher, and his family founded one of the largest publishing houses in seventeenth-century Europe. Merian's father died when she was three, and her mother married still-life artist Jacob Marrel, who specialized in painting flowers. Marrel encouraged Merian to draw, mix paints, and make prints. Merian began formal training under a student of Marrel's. She collected specimens of insects and flowers and created her first paintings of them at age thirteen.

Surrounded as a child by books on natural history and paintings of flowers, Merian was inspired to look closely at insects in her garden and at the silkworms being raised in her town. At the time, it was believed that insects spontaneously generated from rotting meat or fruit. But Merian realized that silkworms and caterpillars produced moths and butterflies. She collected caterpillars to find out how they changed. Merian's interest in insects was unusual as they were considered repugnant and as a result their life cycles were not well understood.

In 1655, Merian married and soon had a daughter. The family moved to Nuremburg five years later. There Merian gave drawing lessons, created designs for embroidery, and published *The New Book of Flowers*,

This beautifully detailed drawing of a Rocu tree of Suriname by Maria Sibylla Merian shows the host plant and the metamorphosis of an insect from egg to caterpillar to pupa to adult moth.

which became a popular artist's reference. Merian continued her study of insects. She also had a second daughter during this time of her life.

Merian was unhappy in her marriage. She left her husband and settled with her daughters in Holland. There she published *Caterpillars, Their Wondrous Transformation and Peculiar Nourishment from Flowers,* or *The Caterpillar Book*, a two-volume book describing details of the life cycles and evolution of the insects she had observed. Merian depicted each stage of a caterpillar changing to a butterfly and the plants the caterpillar ate during this transformation, debunking the theory of spontaneous generation. Merian's book was popular and widely read within her social circle, although her observations were ignored by scientists, in part because the book was written in German rather than in Latin, the official language of science at the time.

Merian received permission from the city of Amsterdam to conduct a self-funded trip to Suriname, a Dutch colony in South America, to study insects. There she classified, described, and illustrated many insects and plants unknown to Europeans. Her classification of moths and butterflies is still used today. Although she planned to stay for five years, she contracted malaria and returned to Europe after two years. In 1705, she published her most important work, *The Insects of Suriname*. She died in Amsterdam in 1717.

Merian's daughters were both artists as well, often collaborating with their mother. Her younger daughter published a collection of her mother's work shortly after Merian's death. Merian's beautiful and meticulous depictions are included in collections and exhibitions around the world.

Mary Anning (1799–1847): British Paleontologist

Mary Anning was born and lived her life in Lyme Regis on the southern coast of England, where the limestone and shale cliffs at the edge of town held fossil treasures for the picking. The area is known today as the Jurassic Coast because of its wealth of dinosaur and marine reptile fossils from the second period of the Mesozoic Era, called the Jurassic period. During this period (from 201.3 million to 145 million years ago), pterosaurs flew in the air, dinosaurs trekked across the land, and other reptiles inhabited the oceans.

Anning's family was working class, and her father supplemented his cabinetry business by collecting fossils to sell to tourists, with the help of his children. He died when Anning was eleven, leaving the family in poverty. Anning, her brother Joseph, and their mother continued the fossil business.

When Anning was twelve, she and her brother gained recognition for one of their finds—a 4-foot (122-centimeter) ichthyosaur skull that Anning chiseled from a rock her brother had found. Anning dug up the rest of the 17-foot- (5-meter) long skeleton a few months later. The finds raised questions about the history of Earth and of living things that ran counter to the Biblical account that Earth is only a few thousand years old.

Anning learned to read and write at Sunday school. She was encouraged to study the new science of geology—the physical structure and history of Earth—by an essay written by the family's pastor. She read whatever scientific literature she could find and dissected animals to gain a better understanding of the anatomy of the animals whose fossils she found. Scientists were beginning to understand that fossils tell the history of Earth and of

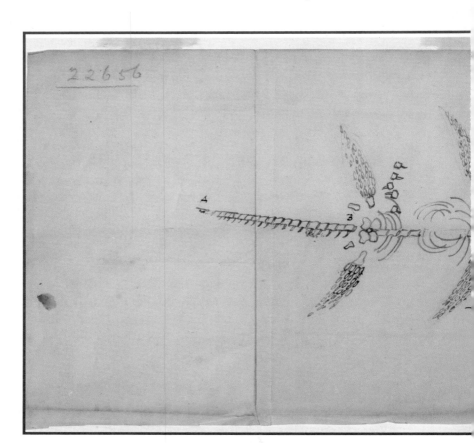

life that existed millions of years ago. This developed into the discipline paleontology, to which Anning was a major contributor.

In 1823, Anning unearthed the first plesiosaur, an ancient long-necked marine reptile, and in 1828, the first British example of a pterosaur, a flying reptile. To support her family, Anning sold many of her fossils to scientists and wealthy collectors after completing

Mary Anning's 1824 drawing shows the first intact fossilized skeleton of a plesiosaur. The ancient reptile lived about 203 million years ago and was unearthed by Anning.

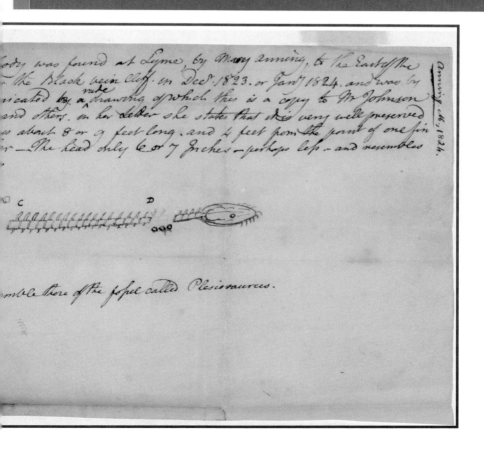

her classification, scientific drawings, and notes. These men often published the finds as their own, and although Anning was rarely given credit for her discoveries, she started to earn a reputation for her ability to find, identify, and classify fossils.

Eventually Anning earned enough money to open a store, Anning's Fossil Depot, attracting fossil collectors and geologists from Europe and the United States. The depth and breadth of her scientific knowledge impressed her customers, who purchased her fossils for museums and private collections. Despite her expertise, Anning was barred from membership in the Geological Society of London because she was a woman. It wasn't until much later in her life that her contributions began to be recognized. By the time of her death from breast cancer at the age of forty-seven, she was held in high regard by members of the Geological Society. Today her accomplishments are highly respected, and she is considered one of the most important scientists in British history.

Dr. Barbara McClintock (1902– 1992): American Geneticist and Nobel Prize Winner

Even as a child, Barbara McClintock was an independent thinker. Her doctor father and homemaker mother didn't understand their daughter. Born in Hartford, Connecticut, in 1902, McClintock

Barbara McClintock is shown here at work at Cold Spring Harbor Laboratory, around the time of her research proving genetic transposition. Her achievement was recognized with a Nobel Prize thirty-five years later.

loved to play baseball with the neighborhood team, but the long skirts girls were required to wear got in her way. She insisted on wearing a pair of "bloomers," loose pants gathered at the ankles that allowed unrestricted movement. In high school, science classes captured McClintock's interest. She insisted that her teacher let her find the answers to problems in her own way. McClintock's parents didn't intend to send their daughters to college, but when McClintock's father returned from World War I, she convinced him to let her attend Cornell University to study biology.

Genetics, or the study of heredity, was a relatively new field of science. Powerful new microscopes led to discoveries about the chromosomes in cells. At Cornell, McClintock studied the chromosomes of maize (corn) and earned her PhD in botany, specializing in cytology, genetics, and zoology, in 1927. She stayed at Cornell, publishing important papers on genetics, including her groundbreaking paper on genetic crossover, a process by which chromosomes exchange information. McClintock worked as an instructor, but the university would not hire her as a professor because she was a woman. McClintock accepted a position as assistant professor at the University of Missouri, where she continued her research.

A brilliant scientific researcher, McClintock was solitary, focused, and sometimes obstinate. After five years, she left Missouri for the Cold Spring Harbor Laboratory in New York, where she stayed for the rest of her career. Until her 1948 discovery, scientists believed that genes stayed fixed in one place on their chromosomes. McClintock proved that genes are not fixed in place, but instead "jump," thus producing variations in the colors

CHROMOSOMAL CROSSOVER

Between 1929 and 1931, while working at Cornell, Barbara McClintock published nine major papers, becoming a recognized leader in the field of genetics. In 1931, McClintock and Harriet Creighton, a PhD student, published a landmark study. McClintock had been researching corn because genetic changes could easily be seen in the color and texture of corn kernels. The study used corn to prove a theory about chromosomal crossover that had previously been useful to geneticists, although no one had actually proven it. The study by Creighton and McClintock proved that during reproduction, genetic material was exchanged between two like chromosomes during meiosis, or cell division. Two chromosomes crossing over each other could be observed under a microscope.

McClintock planted corn kernels that were waxy and purple. Those plants were fertilized with pollen from nonwaxy, nonpurple plants. The new corn plants harvested in the fall were of different types: 1) those with waxy and purple kernels, 2) those with nonwaxy and nonpurple kernels, 3) those with waxy kernels, and 4) those with purple kernels. The researchers concluded that the chromosomal crossing over correlated with genetic crossing over, that is, with different traits.

of corn kernels. She referred to this process as genetic transposition.

McClintock's colleagues considered her work too radical and much of it was ignored until the 1960s and 1970s, when DNA researchers came up with findings similar to McClintock's, confirming her results. Thirty-five years after McClintock produced her research, the scientific community came to understand and recognize her achievements. In 1983, McClintock became the first woman to be the sole winner of the Nobel Prize for Physiology or Medicine.

Rachel Carson (1907–1964): American Biologist

Rachel Carson was born in 1907. Growing up on a farm in Pennsylvania, Carson wanted to be a writer. She was also fascinated with the wildlife she observed in the environment around her. At age ten, she became a published author when *St. Nicholas* magazine for children printed her story about a World War I pilot.

Carson earned a degree in English at Pennsylvania College for Women, attending on a scholarship. Her biology classes interested her as well, and she went on to earn her master's degree in zoology at Johns Hopkins University. She was hired by the United States Bureau of Fisheries to write fifty-two episodes of a radio program called *Romance Under the Waters*. Her literary writing about nature for magazines such as *The Atlantic* led to her first published book, *Under the Sea-Wind*. Her next book, *The Sea Around Us*, was a commercial success, winning the National Book Award. It is still highly regarded. But it was Carson's

Biologist and author Rachel Carson is seen here in the woods near her home around the time of the publication of her influential book, *Silent Spring*.

book *Silent Spring* in 1962 that had the greatest impact on society. In it, Carson took a hard look at the use of chemical pesticides, such as DDT, that were damaging the natural environment.

DDT (dichlorodiphenyltrichloroethane) is a chemical compound developed in the 1940s to combat insects that carry malaria, typhus, and other diseases. It was so effective that it was used on crops, around homes and in gardens, and around farm animals. In the 1950s and 1960s, some insects became resistant to DDT and it lost some of its effectiveness. Animals at the top of the food chain were at risk because of the accumulated effects. In her book, Rachel Carson advocated that pesticides such as DDT ought to be used in a minimal and controlled way. Although the chemical industry waged an expensive campaign to discredit Carson, *Silent Spring* was a best-seller. Through Carson's work, the public began to understand the toxic effects of DDT and became concerned about the dangers of pesticides to humans, to animals, and to the environment.

Rachel Carson died in 1964 of breast cancer, however, her work inspired a shift in the way people think about human effects on the environment. In the 1970s, Congress passed the National Environmental Policy Act, and the Environmental Protection Agency (EPA) was established. Every April, Earth Day celebrations help foster awareness of the importance of protecting the environment. Rachel Carson is regarded as the person who began the environmental movement, not just in the United States but around the world.

Dr. Rita Levi-Montalcini (1909– 2012): Italian Neurobiologist and Nobel Prize Winner

Rita Levi-Montalcini was born into a well-to-do Italian Jewish family in 1909. Against the wishes of her father, she was determined to attend college and dedicate her life to science. Levi-Montalcini decided to become a doctor after a close friend died of stomach cancer. She graduated summa cum laude from medical school and interned at the Institute of Anatomy, studying the development of the nervous system in chick embryos.

In 1938, Fascists—radical authoritarian nationalists—took power in Italy and passed laws prohibiting Jews from pursuing academic and professional careers, including the practice of medicine. Undaunted, Levi-Montalcini left the university and set up a laboratory in her bedroom in the family home in Turin. When the Germans invaded Italy in 1943, her family left Turin and went into hiding in Florence, where they remained, under false identities, until 1945. While in hiding, Levi-Montalcini pursued her interest in how embryonic nerve tissue develops into different types, setting up a lab and purchasing hard to come by eggs from local farmers. She put forward the idea that a special nutrient must

Rita Levi-Montalcini and Stanley Cohen's discovery of the nerve-growth factor produced in the salivary glands of mice paved the way to understanding diseases such as multiple sclerosis and Alzheimer's disease.

cause differentiation of the nerve cells.

When Dr. Viktor Hamburger, professor at Washington University, read Levi-Montalcini's research in 1946, he arranged for a one-semester research fellowship at his lab in St. Louis, Missouri, so they could work together. After duplicating the results of her research, Hamburger offered Levi-Montalcini a permanent position, which she accepted. She stayed there until 1961. It was there, in 1952, after Hamburger's retirement, that Levi-Montalcini did her most important research. Working with Stanley Cohen, Levi-Montalcini isolated the nerve-growth factor (NGF). NGF plays an important role in the growth of nerve cells in the peripheral nervous system, and it was the first of many cell-growth factors to be found. The discovery of the NGF opened the door to combating diseases of the nervous system. Levi-Montalcini and Cohen were granted the Nobel Prize for their work.

Levi-Montalcini thrived in the face of hardship during the 103 years of her life. She did not let anyone stop her from pursuing her research, and she harbored no ill will toward the Italian government after the war. In a 1993 interview in *Scientific American*, Levi-Montalcini said, "If I had not been discriminated against or had not suffered persecution, I would never have received the Nobel Prize."

CHAPTER THREE

WOMEN IN PHYSICS AND CHEMISTRY

P hysics and chemistry look at the tiniest components of life and ask the greatest questions. Why are things what they are? How does the universe work? Women physicists and chemists uncovered the mysteries of radioactive properties of matter, putting their own lives at risk while saving the lives of others. Women chemists continued their research even when their discoveries were initially attributed to male colleagues. Women chemists' inventions ranged from wrinkle-free cotton to life-saving X-ray machines.

Dr. Marie Curie (1867–1934): Polish French Physicist and Chemist and Nobel Prize Winner

Marie Curie was born Maria Salomea Sklodowska in Warsaw, Poland, in 1867. Her father was a teacher of mathematics and physics, and he brought his lab equipment home, introducing his children to the world of physics. Curie was a good student with a remarkable memory, and she won a gold medal upon graduating. The family suffered great financial loss because of a bad investment and their political support for Polish independence from Russia. Curie went to work as a governess, supporting herself and her older sister while she studied medicine in Paris. In turn, her sister allowed Curie to live with her briefly while she studied physics, chemistry, and math at the University of Paris. Curie met her future husband, Pierre Curie, who was an instructor there. They became research colleagues as well as husband and wife.

Curie intended to return to Poland to work in her field, but because she was a woman, she was turned down for a place at Kraków University. She returned to Paris to pursue her PhD. She went on to become the first woman to win a Nobel Prize. Along with her husband and Henri Becquerel, she was awarded the Nobel Prize for Physics in 1903 for their work with uranium and for the discovery of what Curie named radioactivity. Between them, the Curies published thirty-two scientific papers on their results between 1898 and 1902. One paper stated that when exposed to radium, tumor-forming cells were destroyed faster than healthy cells. Much later, this discovery led to radiation treatment for certain types of cancer.

Curie joined the faculty of the École Normale Supérieure, the first woman to do so. She earned

Marie Curie, a Polish-born French physicist and the first woman to win a Nobel Prize, is shown here working in her laboratory around 1910.

her doctorate in 1903. She and her husband worked together until 1906, when Pierre Curie died in a tragic carriage accident. Curie took over her husband's teaching post, becoming the first woman to teach at the Collège de Sorbonne at the University of Paris.

Curie won her second Nobel Prize, this time in chemistry, in 1911 for having isolated pure radium and polonium from pitchblende. She named the element polonium in honor of her country of birth, Poland. She was the director of the Radium Institute, built at the University of Paris in 1914, which became an international center for nuclear physics. She continued working on the uses and collection of radium, having no idea that long-term exposure to radioactivity would ultimately lead to her death.

In 1914, Curie set up France's first military radiology center. Recognizing during World War I that soldiers wounded in battle had the best chance at recovery if treated right away, Curie and her teenage daughter Irène Joliot-Curie, who went on to win her own Nobel Prize, organized mobile X-ray trucks and developed mobile radiography units for use in field hospitals, treating more than one million wounded soldiers with those units.

Despite her many achievements, Curie lived modestly and preferred to avoid the limelight. She gave away most of her Nobel Prize money to family, students, and research associates. She decided against patenting the radium-isolation process she developed so the scientific community could continue to use it easily. She refused several medals and awards. She is considered the most inspirational woman in science.

TOO HOT TO HANDLE

Marie Curie's research notes, papers, and even her cookbook from the 1890s are locked away in lead-lined boxes. These items are considered too dangerous to handle because of the high levels of radioactive contamination. The deleterious effects of long-term exposure to radioactive material were unknown to Curie and her colleagues. Curie routinely carried test tubes holding radioactive isotopes in her pocket. She was also regularly exposed to X-rays while working as a radiologist helping wounded soldiers during World War I. Curie suffered from chronic illness and cataracts that severely hampered her eyesight, but she never publicly acknowledged that these may have been caused by a lifetime of exposure to radiation.

Curie died of leukemia, caused by exposure to radiation, the substance that she spent most of her life studying.

Dr. Irène Joliot-Curie (1897–1956): French Chemist and Nobel Prize Winner

Growing up as the eldest daughter of two exceptional scientists, Irène Joliot-Curie posesses extraordinary

Marie Curie and her daughter Irène Joliot-Curie are shown here. Joliot-Curie won a Nobel Prize thirty-two years after her mother became the first woman to win one.

abilities herself, particularly in math. Her parents, Marie and Pierre Curie, were Nobel Laureates for their work with radium and radioactivity. Joliot-Curie was only nine when her father was killed in a roadway accident, and she always remained protective of and devoted to her brilliant mother.

Joliot-Curie was born in 1897 in Paris, France. She was still in her teens when she went to war. Few hospitals had X-ray equipment in France during the Great War (World War I), and her mother, Marie Curie, developed mobile units to take new life-saving equipment to the battlefields. Joliot-Curie worked as a radiology technician, training medical staff, who were often resistant at first, in how to use the new technology in field hospitals.

Joliot-Curie was a serious and straightforward person. Most people thought of her as aloof because she did not engage in social niceties or polite conversation. She did not like to waste time and was known to carry a book to read in case she became bored with conversation at social events.

Joliot-Curie studied at the Radium Institute, earning her doctorate in 1925. She met and married chemical engineer Frédéric Joliot when he came to work at the Radium Institute, where Irène worked with her mother. Like her parents had been, Irène and her husband were colleagues. Together, the Joliot-Curies discovered the first artificially produced radioactive element. By placing aluminum foil next to polonium, they discovered that the aluminum foil became radioactive. Joliot-Curie won the 1935 Nobel Prize in Chemistry for her work with artificial radioactive elements, sharing the prize with her husband. Joliot-Curie was given the position of professor at the Faculty of Science in Paris. The results of the research led by Joliot-Curie's team into radium nuclei laid the groundwork for a group of German scientists to discover nuclear fission—the splitting of the nucleus, which creates enormous amounts of energy.

Like her mother, Joliot-Curie died from the cumulative effects of exposure to radiation.

Dr. Lise Meitner (1878–1968): Austrian Swedish Physicist

Lise Meitner was born in Vienna, Austria, in 1878, a time when girls were by law prevented from attending the schools that prepared boys for entering the university. Meitner called the years before girls were admitted "lost years," which she felt put her behind in her career, for she desperately wanted to study physics and could not. Her father worried about how she would support herself because she had no interest in marriage. So she earned a teaching certificate and then persuaded her father to pay for a tutor so she could pass the university entrance exams. It took her two years to complete eight years' worth of studies, and she passed the exam in 1901 at the age of twenty-two. Meitner earned a doctorate in physics in 1906, graduating summa cum laude, from the University of Vienna—the second woman to earn that degree in the history of the university.

The beginning of the twentieth century was a heady time for physicists. Their research was leading to exciting new discoveries about the atom. Women were the exception in physics departments and were treated as inferior, but Meitner went to Berlin to study with the renowned physicist Max Planck. Otto Hahn, a young chemist her own age, was studying radioactivity at the Institute of Chemistry in Berlin in 1907. Meitner had been looking for laboratory space to do just that, but women were not allowed in the building. Meitner and Hahn decided to work together as chemist and physicist, and Hahn spoke up for her. Though at the start she had to work in a small room in the basement, Meitner formed a collaborative research team with Hahn that lasted for thirty years and eventually resulted in the discovery of nuclear fission in uranium. Nuclear fission is the process used by nuclear reactors to create heat and therefore electricity, also known as nuclear energy. Nuclear fission is also the foundation for nuclear weapons.

Meitner, a Jew, was the first full professor of physics in Germany. She lost her position as professor at the Kaiser Wilhelm Institute in 1938, when she reluctantly left her work behind to flee Nazi Germany. She went to Sweden and secretly continued corresponding with Hahn about their uranium research. From a distance, she interpreted the results of the experiments that Hahn struggled with. She realized that their work caused atoms to split apart, a process she called fission, and release energy: nuclear energy.

The 1930s were productive years for Lise Meitner. Meitner was a full professor at the Kaiser Wilhelm Institute and recognized as a world-class physicist.

Meitner did not share the Nobel Prize in Chemistry that was awarded for the discovery of nuclear fission. It went to Hahn in 1944. Many people felt that this was an injustice. However, Meitner did receive many honors, including the Enrico Fermi Award in 1966 for the discovery of uranium fission with Otto Hahn and Fritz Strassman. Element 109 was named meitnerium in her honor. The great physicist Albert Einstein acknowledged her brilliance when he called Lise Meitner "the German Madame Curie."

Dr. Rosalind Franklin (1920–1958): British Chemist

As a girl, Rosalind Franklin enjoyed mathematics, and she always knew what she wanted to be—a scientist. She earned a bachelor's degree in physical chemistry from Newnham College, a women's college at Cambridge University, in 1941. She went to work to help the war effort by doing coal research. She earned a PhD in physical chemistry from Cambridge University in 1945, based on her wartime work on the properties of coal. The microstructures of coal that she studied helped set the groundwork for classifying coals and for determining how well they performed.

After the war, Franklin learned X-ray crystallography for analyzing carbons at a laboratory in Paris. When she was awarded a fellowship at King's College London, she returned to England and was asked to use her technique in X-ray crystallography to study

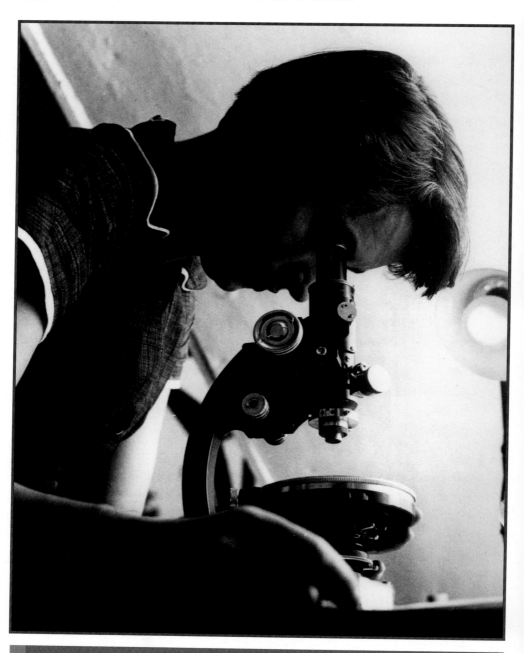

Rosalind Franklin is shown here at work in the 1950s. Her X-ray diffraction studies of DNA molecules were important in the discovery of the structure of DNA.

DNA. Due to a misunderstanding, her colleague Maurice Wilkins had thought he would be the one to study DNA, and because of this, he resented Franklin.

In her crystallography lab, Franklin created a photo that clearly showed DNA as a double helix. Without Franklin's permission, Maurice Wilkins shared the photo with fellow scientists James Watson and Francis Crick, who were also trying to determine the structure of DNA. The rest is history. Watson and Crick were credited with the discovery of the double helix and, along with Wilkins, were awarded the 1962 Nobel Prize in Chemistry without revealing that they had utilized Franklin's work.

Franklin's achievements in coal-chemistry research, the structure of viruses, and the structure of DNA were extensive during her short lifetime. She died of cancer in 1958 at thirty-seven years old, and it was only after her death that the truth about her work in finding the structure of DNA came to light and her achievement was widely recognized.

Dr. Ruth Benerito (1916–2013): American Chemist

Born in 1916 in New Orleans, Louisiana, Ruth Rogan Benerito grew up in a time when most women were not educated in the hard sciences. However, her parents, both college graduates who valued education and women's rights, encouraged Benerito to develop her interests in math and chemistry. Benerito earned

The recipient of highest honors for her work with textiles, Ruth Benerito was also an inspiring teacher. After retiring from the USDA, she taught college chemistry until age eighty-one.

a bachelor of science degree from Newcomb College, the women's college of Tulane University, in 1935. She was one of only two women who were allowed to enroll in chemistry classes at the time. She also received her master's degree in physics at Tulane in 1938. During the Great Depression, Benerito took a job teaching high school. Then, during World War II, she earned her PhD in physical chemistry from the University of Chicago, where many of the best minds in science were teaching. After the war, Benerito taught engineering at Tulane but quit after having been passed over for promotions in favor of her male colleagues multiple times. That led to her career working for the United States Department of Agriculture (USDA).

With her education and inventive mind, Benerito was able to help save the cotton industry when it seemed that competition from wrinkle-free synthetic fabrics would put it out of business. She is credited with developing wash-and-wear cotton fabric that did not require ironing, although she resisted the acclaim, saying in a 2004 interview, "No one person discovered it or is responsible for it, but I contributed to a new process of doing it." As head of the USDA lab in New Orleans, her experiments with a new process of crosslinking the cellulose chains of cotton molecules with other molecules were far in advance of anything that had been done before. This made cotton wrinkle resistant and also led to the development of flame-retardant and stain-resistant cotton fabrics.

There was a resurgence in the use of cotton, thanks to Benerito's work. Her achievement is regarded as one of the most influential technological developments of the late twentieth century. Benerito received the USDA's Distinguished Service Award in 1970, the Lemelson-MIT Lifetime Achievement Award in 2002, and was inducted into the National Inventors Hall of Fame in 2008. She held fifty-five patents.

CHAPTER FOUR

WOMEN AND SPACE

For thousands of years, humans have looked to the skies in wonder. In the last two hundred years, women astronomers, astronauts, and engineers have made significant contributions to the identification, cataloging, and exploration of the stars and planets they were inspired to study. From observing new comets to finding new planets, from cataloging all visible celestial elements to inventing ways to explore them faster, women are working alongside men to understand the universe in which we live.

Maria Mitchell (1818–1889): American Astronomer

Maria Mitchell was one of ten siblings born into a Quaker family on the island of Nantucket,

Massachusetts. Like many Quakers, her parents believed in equal education for all of their children, and Mitchell learned astronomy at her father's knee. William Mitchell was a prominent educator and amateur astronomer, and Mitchell learned to use a telescope to "sweep the heavens" from the rooftop of their home when she was young.

In 1847, Mitchell was a twenty-nine-year-old librarian who studied the stars at night using a two-inch (five-centimeter) telescope. She was poised to become the first professional woman astronomer in the United States. On October 1, she observed a new comet and established its orbit, and this brought her almost instant recognition in scientific circles. The comet was dubbed Miss

Maria Mitchell (*second from left*) is seen here with her astronomy students and a telescope outside the Vassar College Observatory circa 1870. Mitchell was the first astronomy professor and observatory director at Vassar.

Mitchell's Comet and her discovery was publicized internationally. The following year, Mitchell became the first woman elected to the American Academy of Arts and Sciences. The King of Denmark awarded her a gold medal for her discovery of a "telescopic comet," that is, one able to be viewed only through a telescope and not with the naked eye.

When Vassar College, at the time a women's college, opened in 1865, Mitchell was the first professor hired. She was also appointed director of the Vassar College Observatory. Mitchell and her widowed father moved into the observatory's residence. The observatory had state-of-the-art technology and was designed to be both a teaching and research facility. Mitchell's name lent cachet to the new women's college, but more importantly, her teaching and advocacy for her students made her a beloved figure. She defied the college's curfew, which would have denied her students access to the observatory at night—an absurd rule for astronomy students. Her students were allowed into all-male Harvard astronomy classes because she championed their cause to a resistant Harvard professor. Mitchell cofounded the Association for the Advancement of Women in 1873.

Mitchell and her students recorded sunspots photographically and determined that they were not clouds, but whirling vortices. She studied Saturn and Jupiter as well as nebulae, comets, and double stars. When Mitchell and her students traveled across the country to Denver, Colorado, in 1878 to view

ASSOCIATION FOR THE ADVANCEMENT OF WOMEN

In September 1873, Maria Mitchell helped to found the Association for the Advancement of Women (AAW), an organization whose mission was to improve the domestic and social positions of women by providing access to opportunities for their intellectual, moral, and physical development. For the next thirty years, members of the AAW met annually to attend lectures and participate in discussions on topics such as enlightened motherhood, equitable monetary division between husband and wife, higher education for women, the establishment of women in various professions, and women's place in government. Mary A. Livermore served as AAW president in its first year, and Mitchell was elected president each of the following two years.

a total solar eclipse, newspapers reported the presence of women scientists at the event as an unusual occurrence.

Mitchell taught astronomy until 1888 and died in 1889. Today, the Vassar Observatory used by Maria Mitchell stands empty, and her telescope is displayed at the Smithsonian Institution National Museum of

American History. A comet, (Comet Mitchell, 1847 T1), an asteroid, (#1455, Mitchella), and a lunar crater (Mitchell) give enduring testimony to her life and work.

Annie Jump Cannon (1863–1941): American Astronomer

As a child, Annie Jump Cannon climbed through the trap door in the roof of her home in Dover, Delaware, with a book of constellations, a candle, and a notebook, ready to write down what she saw. She shared her mother's fascination with the night sky, and her mother taught Cannon everything she knew about astronomy.

Born in 1863, Cannon was an excellent student, particularly in mathematics. Her parents—her father was a Delaware state senator—encouraged her to pursue higher education. Cannon attended Wellesley College, where she studied physics and astronomy. She graduated as valedictorian and returned to Delaware. She became interested in photography, a newly developed art form, and traveled extensively through Europe taking photographs and writing about the locations she visited.

Around this time, Cannon suffered an illness, believed to be scarlet fever, that resulted in the loss of most of her hearing, making it difficult for her to socialize. She accepted a job as a physics instructor

In 1925, Annie Jump Cannon became the first woman awarded an honorary doctorate by the University of Oxford. Cannon was also the first female officer of the American Astronomical Society.

at Wellesley and took graduate courses in physics and astronomy. She also learned about spectroscopy, the study of visible light dispersed based on its wavelength through a prism.

To gain access to a more powerful telescope, Cannon enrolled at Radcliffe College. Radcliffe was located near Harvard College (now Harvard University) in Cambridge, Massachusetts. Being a Radcliffe student gave Cannon access to the Harvard College Observatory, where she was ultimately offered a position working for Edward Pickering, the director of the observatory. Pickering's goal was to map and define every star visible to a "photographic magnitude"—the brightness of a photographed object—of nine. Using a prism, a telescope, a camera, and a magnifying glass, Cannon studied photographs of the night sky and classified the stars according to the spectrum of light they gave off as visible in the photographs. She refined the classification system (O, B, A, F, G, K, or M) and catalogued more than three hundred thousand stars. Her work on both *The Henry Draper Catalogue* (1918–1924) and *The Henry Draper Extension* (1925–1949), which classified even fainter stars than magnitude nine, was vast and both volumes, as well as her classification system, are still in use today.

Cannon characterized her work not as the product of genius, but of patience. By any measure, her skills in cataloguing the entire sky were remarkable and the effects long lasting. Cannon was awarded an honorary doctor of science from Oxford University and an honorary membership in the then all-male Royal Astronomical Society. In 1933, Cannon established an award to encourage women researchers in the field of astronomy. The Annie Jump Cannon Award is given by the American Astronomical Society annually to a female astronomer for outstanding research done and as an encouragement of future research.

Yvonne Brill (1924–2013): Canadian American Rocket Engineer

Yvonne Brill was born in 1924 in Manitoba, Canada, to Belgian immigrant parents, neither of whom had a high school education. Her childhood inspiration was the famous female aviation pioneer Amelia Earhart. Passing by the University of Manitoba on a streetcar, ten-year-old Brill decided she wanted to go to college there someday. In high school, Brill did well in math and physics, but girls were not encouraged to pursue those fields. In an interview with the Society of Women Engineers, Brill remembered a male physics teacher who "just felt that women would never get anywhere." Because the University of Manitoba did not allow women into the engineering program, Brill studied mathematics and chemistry and graduated at the top of her

Yvonne Brill is awarded the National Medal of Technology and Innovation by President Barack Obama in 2011. The award recognized Brill's innovative work in jet propulsion systems for communication satellites.

class. She accepted a job in California, where she worked on the design of the first American satellite.

Brill was a brilliant rocket engineer known for her work with propulsion systems for satellites. Her career took her across the United States and back, working on rocket designs for the National Aeronautics and Space Administration (NASA) moon missions and the *Mars Observer* as well as developing an efficient electrothermal hydrazine thruster used in satellites. Her invention, the hydrazine resistojet propulsion system, for which she holds the patent, became the industry standard.

Brill often met with gender discrimination, but she never let it prevent her from doing the work at which she excelled. She is quoted as saying she chose to enter the field of rocket engineering because she knew she would be the only woman, and she figured that "they would not invent rules to discriminate against one person." She frequently encouraged girls and young women to learn about math and to become engineers.

Brill was the recipient of many awards and honors, including the NASA Distinguished Public Service Medal and the National Medal of Technology and Innovation, awarded by President Barack Obama in 2011. Brill's family life was important to her. She moved to accommodate her husband's jobs and took off eight years to raise three children. However, a *New York Times* obituary at the time of her death in 2013 that opened with a description of her family life and culinary skill before mentioning her achievements as a rocket engineer drew such criticism that it was revised.

Dr. Valentina Tereshkova (1937–): Russian Cosmonaut and Engineer

At twenty-four years old, Valentina Tereshkova was chosen to train in secrecy as a Soviet cosmonaut. At the time, she was a worker in a textile factory, with considerable skill as an amateur parachute jumper. Born in 1937 in central Russia to working-class parents, Tereshkova was physically fit, had a reputation for being a good worker, and her father had been a war hero killed in action. She was the perfect choice to promote the Soviet Union's burgeoning space program.

Inspired by the 1961 spaceflight of Russian cosmonaut Yuri Gagarin, the chief rocket engineer for the Soviet Union proposed putting a woman into space. Four hundred women applied for the opportunity. After passing rigorous exams and enduring intense physical training, five women were selected. Tereshkova was the strongest candidate and the only one to fly. She was a skilled skydiver, personable, and a model worker, a trait the Soviet government wanted to promote to the public.

On June 16, 1963, Tereshkova became the first woman to travel in space, completing forty-eight orbits around the Earth in seventy-one hours aboard the spacecraft *Vostok 6*. In that single flight, Tereshkova spent more time in space than all of the American astronauts who had flown to date combined. Although she was nauseous for most of the flight, she took photographs of the horizon and kept a flight log. She manually controlled her landing back on Earth after repairing problems with the spacecraft's programming.

Tereshkova became a role model for a new generation of Soviet girls interested in careers in science and technology. However, it wasn't until 1982, when competition with the US space program provided the impetus to send another woman into space, that Svetlana Savitskaya became the second woman in space. American astronaut Sally Ride flew on the space shuttle *Challenger* in June 1983, thus becoming the first American woman in space.

Inspired by her flight, Tereshkova went on to earn her degree as a cosmonaut engineer and a doctorate in engineering. She served in several Soviet government positions, received numerous awards, and, despite the demise of the Soviet Union, is considered a hero throughout Russia. On her seventieth birthday, she offered to fly to Mars even if it would be a one-way trip.

Dr. Ellen Ochoa (1958–): Hispanic American Astronaut

Ellen Ochoa was born in 1958 in Los Angeles and grew up in La Mesa, California. As a girl, she enjoyed studying math and music in school and was an outstanding student. Ochoa says, "My mom expected us to work hard and do well." An accomplished flutist, Ochoa thought she might pursue a career in music, but her friends in calculus class were majoring in science and engineering, and she decided to pursue a physics major. She earned a bachelor of science degree in physics from San Diego State University and went on to Stanford University for a master of science degree as well as a doctorate in electrical engineering. Working as a research engineer there and later at Sandia National Laboratories and the National Aeronautics and Space Administration (NASA) Ames Research Center, she helped to develop three patented optical systems and methods.

In 1985, Ochoa applied to NASA to become an astronaut but wasn't selected. In 1987, however, she applied again and was one of 120 people chosen out of thousands of applicants. She was selected as a NASA astronaut for the class of 1990.

In 1993, Ochoa rode the space shuttle *Discovery* on a nine-day mission, becoming the first Hispanic woman to fly in space. Three more missions followed, for a total of 978 hours in space. Ochoa operated

Taking a break from her busy day in space, astronaut Ellen Ochoa plays flute selections for her fellow crewmembers on the space shuttle *Discovery* in 1993.

the Remote Manipulator System (RMS) robotic arm on her space missions. As mission specialist on her first flight, she used it to deploy a satellite to study the sun's corona. On her second flight, she used the RMS to retrieve an atmospheric research satellite that studied the sun. In 1999, a ten-day mission was the first to dock with the International Space Station. She operated the RMS during an eight-hour spacewalk. On her fourth mission, the RMS was used to move spacewalking astronauts around outside the space station.

Ochoa was appointed head of the Johnson Space Center in 2012—the first Hispanic director and the second female director. Besides being the home of NASA's astronaut corps, the Johnson Space Center is a hub of scientific and technological learning. The center encourages students to pursue STEM fields through several of its programs. No fewer than six schools in the United States are named for her, and she was inducted into the US Astronaut Hall of Fame in 2017.

Dr. Sara Seager (1971–): Canadian American Astronomer

Sara Seager was born in Toronto, Canada, and grew up there. Always fascinated by the stars, one of her fondest memories is of attending a "star party" and looking through a telescope. Seager credits her toughness in part to being the child of divorced parents. She attended a high school recognized for its science curriculum.

Seager's physician father tried to discourage his exceptional daughter from becoming an astronomer, urging her instead to be a physician or lawyer. But Seager was determined, studying mathematics and physics, and earning a bachelor of science degree at the University of Toronto, and her doctorate in astronomy from Harvard.

Seager has the heart of an explorer and an eye for exoplanets. She is an astrophysicist and planetary scientist at the Massachusetts Institute of Technology (MIT). She is searching for exoplanets—planets orbiting stars other than our sun—and her goal is to find a planet similar to Earth. She describes her search as looking for "Goldilocks planets—not too big, not too small, not too hot, not too cold, but just right for life." The study of exoplanets is a new field, and Seager is leading the way with her theoretical research. Her theories led to the study of light passing through the atmospheres of exoplanets in order to search for gases such as oxygen that indicate life. Since the mid-1990s, her pioneering theories have resulted in a huge increase in knowledge about exoplanet atmospheres.

The number of confirmed exoplanet discoveries at the beginning of 2018 stood at 3,728. The Kepler space telescope found an exoplanet a little larger than Earth in 2014. The planet Kepler-186f is in its star's Goldilocks zone, and it was the first one

Speaking at a press conference in 2009, Sara Seager presents early findings of the Kepler space telescope launched by NASA earlier that year.

of more than three hundred found orbiting other stars. As these discoveries continue, they increase Seager's resolve to find another Earth.

One of her most important projects is called the Starshade, which is designed to work in tandem with a space telescope to shade the light of a star, enabling astronomers to see what is around the star. Among her numerous awards and honors, Seager was elected to membership in the National Academy of Sciences in 2015 and was chosen to receive what is popularly known as a genius grant as a MacArthur Fellow in 2013.

CHAPTER
FIVE

WOMEN IN MATH AND TECHNOLOGY

M athematics, or the study of quantity, structure, space, and change, is essential in many other fields, such as engineering, chemistry, medicine, physics, and technology. Mathematicians look for patterns and use them to create theories, which they then prove or disprove. Women have made some of the most significant contributions in applied, or practical, mathematics and in pure mathematics, or math for its own sake. Ada Lovelace wrote the first algorithm to be used by a computing machine, becoming the world's first computer programmer. Grace Murray Hopper wrote the first computer language. Emmy Noether made several landmark contributions to theoretical physics and abstract algebra. The "hidden figures" Dorothy Vaughan, Katherine Johnson, and Mary Jackson used their expertise in mathematics to further the space race. And Maryam Mirzakhani's

work in blending dynamics with geometry earned her the Fields Medal, one of the most prestigious awards in the field of mathematics.

Hypatia of Alexandria (ca. 350–415 CE): Astronomer and Mathematician

Hypatia of Alexandria, Egypt, was the daughter of Theon of Alexandria, a leading mathematician and astronomer. Theon was known for his edition of Euclid's *Elements*, which was widely used by scholars until the nineteenth century. Hypatia was educated by her father in astronomy, mathematics, and Greek philosophy. She in turn became the most renowned astronomer and mathematician of her time. Hypatia was also an expert in philosophy. Hypatia became not only a powerful symbol of learning and science, but also a symbol of intellectual pursuit in contrast to religious prejudice. Hypatia lived during turbulent times for Alexandria, when Christians, Jews, and pagan factions were engaging in violent conflicts. The philosophy and customs of ancient Greece were regarded as pagan. Hypatia was a victim of mob violence. She was brutally tortured and murdered by extremist Christians because of her Neoplatonist philosophy. She was a highly regarded teacher of astronomy and of Neoplatonic philosophy, a school of thought derived from Plato's philosophy. People traveled for miles to hear her lectures. Hypatia's

writings, composed of commentaries on the works of others in geometry, astronomy, and number theory, have been lost. It is possible, however, that some of her writings survive under her father's name.

Ada Lovelace (1815–1852): British Mathematician

Ada Lovelace was born Augusta Ada Byron, the daughter of a mathematician named Annabella Milbanke Byron and the poet Lord Byron. Lord Byron was famous for his Romantic poetry and romantic exploits, and her mother became fed up with his impulsive behavior by the time Ada was five weeks old. The Byrons separated and Lovelace grew up without her father. To inhibit any impulsiveness the girl may have inherited from her father, her mother saw to Ada's education in serious subjects such as mathematics and logic. Lovelace later studied with the first professor of mathematics at the University of London, Augustus De Morgan. She married a baron who later became an earl, giving her the title of Countess of Lovelace.

When Lovelace was in her teens, she met the inventor Charles Babbage. She was fascinated by his Difference Engine, which was a mechanical calculator. Although she wanted to study with him right away, it wasn't until later that she caught his attention. When she read a paper about another of his inventions, the Analytical Machine, she saw a connection between

This watercolor portrait by Alfred Edward Chalon shows Ada Lovelace. The stylish countess is known as a computer pioneer; the modern-day computer language Ada was named in her honor.

this machine and factory textile looms. Lovelace translated the paper from French and annotated it in detail. She described how the Analytical Machine could be programmed using punch cards. She commented, "The Analytical Engine weaves algebraic patterns, just as the Jacquard-loom weaves flowers and leaves." She explained how the Analytical Engine could compute Bernoulli numbers. Her work impressed Babbage, and they became friends.

Babbage's plans for a mechanical computer were a forerunner to modern digital computers. Modern mathematical historians have constructed Babbage's computer according to his plans and operated it. Today, Lovelace is known as the first computer programmer. The US military named a computer program Ada in Lovelace's honor. The second Tuesday in October is commemorated as Ada Lovelace Day in honor of her and of the achievements of women in STEM.

Dr. Emmy Noether (1882–1935): German Mathematician

Emmy Noether was born in Erlangen, Germany, in 1882. Her father, Max Noether, was a mathematics professor at the university in Erlangen. Because girls were not permitted to attend the schools that prepared boys for the university, she went to finishing school and earned a teaching certificate. Although she couldn't enroll at the university, she sat in on classes and passed all the exams. Noether then enrolled at the University of Gottingen for graduate study. Later, when women were admitted at Erlangen, she earned her PhD in mathematics there.

Noether worked at the Mathematical Institute of Erlangen from 1907 until 1915 without pay or an official title. These were the conditions for her to be able to work there. However, she made a name for herself, published several papers, and was recognized as brilliant by everyone who worked with her. Her male students were proud to be known as "Noether's boys." Her work focused on mathematical invariants, that is, numbers that remain unchanged when transformations are applied to them.

After seven years, Noether was recruited by prominent mathematicians David Hilbert and Felix Klein at the Mathematical Institute in Gottingen to work on Albert Einstein's general theory of relativity, which had been published in 1915. Noether applied some of her work to Einstein's theory and in the process developed what is known as Noether's Theorem. Einstein called it "penetrating mathematical thinking." Eventually, Noether was given a paid position, though she earned the lowest salary for professors. During the 1920s, Noether worked in abstract algebra on concepts of groups and rings. Her work with symmetry and conservation of energy developed new connections between time and energy.

In 1933, with the rise of Nazism in Germany, Noether was one of the first professors to be fired because she was Jewish. Heeding the encouragement

Emmy Noether gave the world one of the most powerful theorems in physics. Noether's Theorem says that for every symmetry, there is a corresponding conservation law.

of friends who feared for her life, she accepted a position at Bryn Mawr College in the United States. She enjoyed the enthusiasm of her students and colleagues and was happy at Bryn Mawr, but she died unexpectedly two years later at the age of fifty-three. In a letter to the editor of the *New York Times*, Albert Einstein praised Noether: "In the judgment of the most competent living mathematicians, Fraulein Noether was the most significant creative mathematical genius thus far produced since the higher education of women began."

Rear Admiral Dr. Grace Murray Hopper (1906–1992): American Computer Scientist

Grace Murray was born in New York City in 1906. Her great-grandfather was an admiral. Her mother loved math, and her father worked in insurance. Murray was a curious child who took apart alarm clocks to see what made them work. Her early curiosity about machines (including her father's calculator) and her head for mathematics led her to the emerging field of computer science.

Hopper graduated from Vassar College in 1928 with a degree in mathematics and went on to graduate school at Yale, where she earned an MA in 1930 and a PhD in 1934. She was one of a small number of women to earn PhDs in mathematics at the time. She joined the faculty at Vassar and in 1941

Grace Murray Hopper understood that computers had to be user friendly if they were to be widely used. Toward that end, she promoted the Common Business-Oriented Language (COBOL).

was promoted to associate professor of mathematics and physics. When the United States entered World War II, Hopper tried to enlist in the Navy, but she was rejected. According to the Navy, Hopper was too old and underweight, and her expertise was needed at Vassar. Hopper persisted and after three tries she got into the US Naval Reserve.

The Navy assigned Hopper to the Mark I, the first computer. It was a noisy behemoth that stood 8 feet (2.4 meters) high and was 51 feet (15.5 m) long in a basement room at Harvard. The Mark I ran twenty-four hours a day and was capable of computing ballistics. Late in the war, it was used to calculate equations for the atomic explosions of the Manhattan Project. Her commanding officer told her to write a book about the computer, so she wrote the first computer manual.

One of Hopper's greatest contributions to computing was her compiler, which translated computer code into familiar language. Programming was quicker using a compiler, and it helped programmers to think more clearly. Instead of a string of binary code using 1s and 0s, a letter or word was used to instruct the computer. Developing her compiler led to working with a team that created the first computer language, COBOL. This language is still used today.

Hopper retired from the Navy in 1971, but they couldn't do without her for long. In 1972, she was asked to come out of retirement, and in 1985 she was appointed to the rank of rear admiral. In 1986, after her second retirement, Hopper continued to work as a consultant and lecturer. She also appeared on TV talk shows. In 1991, she was the first woman to receive the National Medal of Technology and Innovation. When she died in 1992, Rear Admiral Grace Murray Hopper was given a burial with full naval honors. She was posthumously awarded the Presidential Medal of Freedom in 2016 by President Barack Obama.

Hidden Figures: Dorothy Vaughan, Katherine Johnson, and Mary Jackson

The Oscar-nominated 2016 film *Hidden Figures* tells the story of three pioneering African American women who had careers at the National

A COMPUTER BUG

While working on the Mark II computer, Grace Hopper's team discovered a problem: the computer had a bug. A moth had made its way into one of the components. After they removed the moth, the "debugging" was recorded in the log and the moth was taped to the page. The log with the moth is in the collection of the Smithsonian's National Museum of American History.

Aeronautics and Space Administration (NASA) in its early days, during what is known as the space race. Dorothy Vaughan, Mary Jackson, and Katherine Johnson worked as "human computers," calculating aeronautical research data. These women overcame segregation and discrimination to pave the way for diversity in the sciences.

The mathematician Dorothy Vaughan (née Johnson) was born in Kansas City, Missouri, in 1910. A bright child, she learned to read before she started school. Her family moved to Morgantown, West Virginia, she was seven. Schools there and in other parts of the United States then were racially segregated, and she attended black schools. She was valedictorian of her high school class and won a scholarship to Wilberforce University, where she majored in math. After graduation, Vaughan taught math until World War II opened up other jobs for women and blacks. To support her family, Dorothy Vaughan took a job at Langley Research Center in 1943. It paid more than twice as much as a black teacher's salary. Her job calculating aeronautical research data aided the development of new aircraft for the war. Langley was over a hundred miles from Vaughan's home, and Vaughan commuted via public transportation. In the early 1950s, Vaughan became the first African American female manager at Langley, when she was given the title of section head and was responsible for supervising the computer pool. Later, she became an expert computer programmer at NASA.

Born in 1921, the aeronautical engineer Mary Jackson grew up in Hampton, Virginia. Like Dorothy Vaughan, she studied math in college and then worked as a teacher. When her son was old enough to attend school, Jackson went to work for Vaughan in the computer pool at Langley, calculating how to design aircraft that flew faster than the speed of sound. In the 1950s, there was segregation in the workplace at Langley. Jackson and her colleagues

Mathematician Katherine Johnson was reliably accurate. Her calculations helped synchronize the Apollo Lunar Lander with the Command Module that brought astronauts Neil Armstrong and Buzz Aldrin home from the moon in 1969.

faced segregation in the computer pools, ate at segregated cafeteria tables, and used segregated restrooms. After two years, Jackson moved to an engineering group and had the opportunity to train as an engineer. In 1958, she became NASA's first black female engineer.

Katherine Johnson was born in 1918. She was a brilliant mathematics student who received early promotions and attended the high school of West Virginia State College. She continued there in college, earning highest honors upon graduation in 1937, and took a teaching job. She began working for Dorothy Vaughan at the National Advisory Committee for Aeronautics (NACA) at Langley in 1953. When NACA became the National Aeronautics and Space Administration (NASA) in 1958, Johnson worked for the new space program. In 1961, she calculated trajectories for the flight of *Freedom 7*, which was piloted by Alan Shepard, America's first man in space. She was also the first woman to receive credit for writing a research report at NASA. In 1962, when John Glenn flew *Friendship 7* into space and orbited the Earth, electronic computers were used to control the trajectory of his capsule. However, before taking off, Glenn requested that Johnson make the same calculations by hand, to be sure they were correct. In later years, Johnson did calculations for the Lunar Lander, the Space Shuttle, and the Earth Resources Satellite. Katherine Johnson was awarded the Presidential Medal of Freedom by President Barack Obama, and in 2017, at the age of ninety-nine she attended the dedication of the Katherine G. Johnson Computational Research Facility building at Langley.

Dr. Maryam Mirzakhani (1977–2017): Iranian Mathematician

As a young girl growing up in Iran, Maryam Mirzakhani loved to read and wanted to become a writer. Eventually, though, she discovered that her true passion was for mathematics. She became fascinated with math when her older brother suggested that she add up the numbers from 1 to 100. In high school, she entered an international mathematics competition and won gold medals two years in a row.

Mirzakhani received a bachelor's degree from Sharif University of Technology (Tehran, Iran) in 1999 and went on to graduate school at Harvard University in the United States, where she earned her doctorate in 2004. She taught at Princeton and then at Stanford University until her death in 2017. Mirzakhani was the first woman to win one of the most prestigious honors in mathematics, the Fields Medal, in 2014. The Fields Medal is awarded every four years to between two and four people who are under the age of forty. It recognizes outstanding achievement and is meant to encourage future work. Before Mirzakhani, the medal had been awarded to fifty-two men. She accepted the award with humility and hoped that

Maryam Mirzakhani holds the Fields Medal, awarded to her in August 2014, by the International Mathematical Union, which promotes international cooperation in mathematics. The Fields is among the highest honors in mathematics.

others would be encouraged by her achievement to pursue mathematics.

Mirzakhani's work involves problems related to hyperbolic geometry, describing the dynamics of abstract curved surfaces. Her equations are highly complex, and she found a new proof that related to string theory. Her young daughter described Mirzakhani's method of working as "painting," because Mirzakhani drew her ideas on large sheets of white paper. Mirzakhani characterized her own working style as "slow" mathematics, but others have called it "deep thinking."

Curtis McMullen, a Harvard professor who worked closely with Mirzakhani, describes her achievements in *Scientific American*: "Her work opens new frontiers of research that are just starting to be explored. She approached new mathematics with fearless ambition . . . Her incisive questions shaped the field . . . and will continue to shape it." Mirzakhani is an inspiration to many young women in the field of mathematics. She died in 2017, at the age of forty.

2600 BCE	Chief Physician Merit Ptah is the first female physician in recorded history.
400 CE	Hypatia of Alexandria is the first female mathematician in recorded history.
1849	Elizabeth Blackwell overcomes gender discrimination to become the first woman to graduate from medical school in the United States.
1903	Marie Curie is the first woman to win a Nobel Prize.
1917	Marie Curie trains technicians to use mobile X-ray units in field hospitals during World War I.
1920	Women in the United States gain the right to vote.
1944	The first computer manual is written by Grace Murray Hopper for the Harvard Mark I.
1952	An X-ray photo taken in Rosalind Franklin's lab of a DNA molecule reveals the double helix structure.
1963	Valentina Tereshkova becomes the first woman to fly in space.
2014	Maryam Mirzakhani is the first woman awarded the Fields Medal for mathematics.
2017	The Katherine G. Johnson Computational Research Facility is dedicated at Langley Research Center in Virginia, honoring one of NASA's African American female mathematicians.
2017	According to the World Economic

Forum, women earn only a third of
undergraduate STEM degrees.

2024   The United States Bureau of Labor Statistics
projects there will be well over a million
new and replacement job openings in STEM
occupations between 2014 and 2024.

GLOSSARY

Apgar score The scoring system used to assess the condition of newborns by adding points (0 to 2) for a baby's appearance (skin coloration), pulse (heart rate), grimace (reflexes), activity (muscle tone), and respiration (breathing rate and effort).

chromosomes The threadlike strands in the nucleus of a living cell that carry genes and determine heredity.

compiler A computer program that converts instructions from one computer language to another.

corona The glow around the sun caused by gases and visible during a solar eclipse.

double helix A spiral structure of two parallel strands that coil around an axis, describing the shape of a DNA molecule.

electrothermal hydrazine thruster A type of rocket propulsion system using hydrazine as a propellant.

embryo A developing offspring that has not yet hatched or been born.

exoplanet A planet outside of our solar system, orbiting a star other than our sun.

genes The units of heredity located on chromosomes that control traits passed from parent to offspring.

genetics The study of heredity in plants and animals.

hyperbolic geometry Complex non-Euclidean geometry of curving surfaces.

malaria A recurring tropical fever caused by a parasite that infects people's red blood cells and is transmitted by mosquito bite.

Nobel Prize One of seven annual prizes awarded for outstanding work in the fields of literature, physics, chemistry, physiology or medicine, economics, and peace.

nuclear fission The splitting of the nucleus of an atom into two nuclei, which releases energy.

paleontologist A scientist who studies geology and especially fossils to learn about the past.

physicist An expert who studies the matter and energy present in nature.

pitchblende A black, pitchlike mineral ore that is mined for uranium and radium.

radioactivity Energy that is emitted by unstable isotopes of an element as they decay over time.

STEM An acronym for science, technology, engineering, and mathematics.

spectroscopy The study of the visible spectrum of light from a star as it is dispersed through a prism.

string theory A developing theory in physics that is based on the idea that subatomic particles are stringlike.

X-ray An electromagnetic wave that can pass through the human body and produce a photographic image of the body's interior.

FOR MORE INFORMATION

American Medical Women's Association (AMWA)
1100 E. Woodfield Road
Suite 350
Schaumburg, IL 60173
(847) 517-2801
Email: associatedirector@amwa-doc.org
Website: https://www.amwa-doc.org/about-amwa
The AMWA is a professional organization that focuses
on initiatives to improve the health of women and
children, providing local, national, and international
leadership, advocacy, and education.

Association for Women Geoscientists (AWG)
12000 N. Washington Street, Suite 285
Thornton, CO 80241-3134
(303) 412-6219
Email: office@awg.org
Website: http://www.awg.org
The AWG supports women in the geosciences
by exchanging educational and technical
information and enhancing professional growth
and advancement, as well as listing employment
opportunities in the geosciences. The group
sponsors field trips to geologic areas of interest,
such as a trip to Lyme Regis on the coast of
England in 2018.

Association for Women in Mathematics (AWM)
11240 Waples Mill Road
Suite 200
Fairfax, Virginia 22030
(703) 934-0163
Email: awm@awm-math.org
Website: https://sites.google.com/site/awmmath
    /home
The AWM encourages girls and women to study and
    seek careers in mathematics and promotes their
    equal treatment in the mathematical sciences.
    AWM offers research and mentoring travel grants.

Association for Women in Science (AWIS)
1667 K Street NW
Suite 800
Washington, DC 20006
(202) 588-8175
Email: awis@awis.org
Website: https://www.awis.org
The AWIS sponsors and disseminates research
    to broaden the participation of women and
    minorities in the sciences and promotoes
    equitable scientific workplaces.

Federation of Medical Women of Canada (FMWC)
1021 Thomas Spratt Place
Ottawa (ON) Canada K1G 5L5
(613) 569-5881 or (877) 771-3777
Email: fmwcmain@fmwc.ca
Website https://fmwc.ca

The FMWC is the national organization for Canadian female physicians, encouraging ongoing education, influencing health care policies related to women, providing networking opportunities, and advocating for women's health.

Society for Canadian Women in Science and Technology
#311-525 Seymour Street
Vancouver, BC V6B 3H7
(604) 893-8657
Email: resourcecentre@scwist.ca
Website: http://www.scwist.ca
Members of this society help inspire girls to study and consider scientific careers, boost early career women, and work with partners to support women and strengthen community relationships.

Society of Women Engineers
130 East Randolph Street
Suite 3500
Chicago, IL 60601
(877) 793-4636
Email: hq@swe.org
Website: http://societyofwomenengineers.swe.org /about-swe
The Society of Women Engineers encourages women to reach their potential as engineers and as leaders, providing opportunities to train and network, as well as earn scholarships and advocate.

FOR FURTHER READING

Conkling, Winifred. *Radioactive! How Irène Curie & Lise Meitner Revolutionized Science and Changed the World.* Chapel Hill, NC: Algonquin Young Readers, 2016.

Faulkner, Nicholas, ed. *Top 101 Women of STEM.* New York, NY: Britannica Educational Publishing, 2017.

Freedman, Jeri. *Women of the Scientific Revolution* (Leaders of the Scientific Revolution). New York, NY: Rosen Publishing, 2018.

Gibson, Karen Bush. *Women in Space: 23 Stories of First Flights, Scientific Missions, and Gravity-Breaking Adventures.* Chicago, IL: Chicago Review Press, 2014.

Ignotofsky, Rachel. *Women in Science: 50 Fearless Pioneers Who Changed the World.* Berkeley, CA: Ten Speed Press, 2016.

Jahren, Hope. *Lab Girl.* New York, NY: Alfred A. Knopf, 2016.

Lowery, Zoe. *Social Roles and Stereotypes* (Women in the World). New York, NY: Rosen Publishing, 2018.

Lowery, Zoe. *Women's Rights at Work* (Women in the World). New York, NY: Rosen Publishing, 2018.

Maggs, Sam. *Wonder Women: 25 Innovators, Inventors, and Trailblazers Who Changed History.* Philadelphia, PA: Quirk Books, 2016.

Saujani, Reshma. *Girls Who Code: Learn to Code and Change the World*. New York, NY: Viking, 2017.

Shetterly, Margot Lee. *Hidden Figures* (Young Readers' Edition). New York, NY: HarperCollins Publishers, 2016.

Swaby, Rachel. *Headstrong: 52 Women Who Changed Science—and the World*. New York, NY: Broadway Books, 2015.

Tyson, Neil deGrasse. *Astrophysics for People in a Hurry*. New York, NY: W. W. Norton & Company, 2017.

BIBLIOGRAPHY

Alvord, Lori Arviso, and Elizabeth Cohen Van Pelt. *The Scalpel and the Silver Bear: The First Navajo Woman Surgeon Combines Western Medicine and Traditional Healing.* New York, NY: Bantam Books, 1999.

Brill, Yvonne. "Interview with the Society of Women Engineers." By Deborah Rice, November 3, 2005. http://ethw.org/Oral-History:Yvonne_Brill.

Central Intelligence Agency (CIA). "Suriname." *The World Factbook* online. https://www.cia.gov /library/publications/the-world-factbook/geos /ns.html.

Clausen, Carol, curator. *Elizabeth Blackwell: That girl there is doctor of medicine*. Online exhibit. US National Library of Medicine, National Institutes of Health. Updated July 18, 2013. https://www.nlm .nih.gov/exhibition/blackwell/index.html.

Galvin, Gaby. "NASA's Ellen Ochoa: We Are Going Deeper into Space Than Ever." *US News and World Report*, May 4, 2017. https://www.usnews .com/news/stem-solutions/articles/2017-05-04 /johnson-space-centers-ellen-ochoa-future-of -spaceflight-depends-on-stem-innovation-education.

Holloway, Marguerite. "Finding the Good in the Bad: A Profile of Rita Levi-Montalcini." *Scientific American*, December 30, 2012. https://www .scientificamerican.com/article/finding-the-good -rita-levi-montalcini.

Jones, Chris. "The Woman Who Might Find Us Another Earth." *New York Times Magazine*,

December 7, 2016. https://www.nytimes
.com/2016/12/07/magazine/the-world-sees-me
-as-the-one-who-will-find-another-earth.html.

Lamb, Evelyn. "Mathematics World Mourns Maryam
Mirzakhani, Only Woman to Win Fields Medal."
Scientific American, July 17, 2017. https://www
.scientificamerican.com/article/mathematics
-world-mourns-maryam-mirzakhani-only-woman-to
-win-fields-medal.

National Museum of Nuclear Science & History.
Pioneers of the Atom, interactive exhibit.
Albuquerque, New Mexico. Visited August 31,
2017.

Reynolds, Moira Davison. *American Women Scientists:
23 Inspiring Biographies, 1900–2000.* Jefferson,
NC: McFarland & Company, Inc., Publishers, 1999.

Seager, Sara. "The search for planets beyond our
solar system." TED talk, March, 2015. https://
www.ted.com/talks/sara_seager_the_search_for
_planets_beyond_our_solar_system.

Tereshkova, Valentina. *Valentina Tereshkova,
the First Lady of Space: In Her Own Words.*
SpaceHistory101.com Press, 2015.

Todd, Kim. *Chrysalis: Maria Sibylla Merian and the Secrets
of Metamorphosis.* Orlando, FL: Harcourt, 2007.

Wulf, Andrea. "The Woman Who Made Science
Beautiful." *The Atlantic*, January 19, 2016.
https://www.theatlantic.com/science
/archive/2016/01/the-woman-who-made-science
-beautiful/424620.

INDEX

About the Author

Barbara Allman has written extensively for the educational market, including biographies for young readers. Her special interests are STEM topics and the arts. Prior to her writing career, Allman earned her K–8 teacher certification in Michigan with an additional endorsement in ninth-grade science and taught for ten years. She holds a master of arts in teaching from Oakland University. Allman and her husband live in New Mexico, where people perform scientific research in places such as the Very Large Array Radio Telescope facility, Spaceport America, the National Museum of Nuclear Science and History, and Rockhound State Park.

Photo Credits

Cover, p. 75 NASA; p. 7 Jonas Ekstromer/AFP/Getty Images; p. 10 The Metropolitan Museum of Art, Rogers Fund, 1908; p. 14 Library of Congress Prints and Photographs Division; pp. 16–17 KGPA Ltd /Alamy Stock Photo; pp. 20, 88 Science History Images/Alamy Stock Photo; pp. 24, 35, 58 © AP Images; p. 29 Digital image courtesy of the Getty's Open Content Program, Gift of Tania Norris; pp. 32–33 The Natural History Museum/Alamy Stock Photo; p. 39 Alfred Eisenstaedt/The LIFE Picture Collection/Getty Images; pp. 42–43 Mondadori Portfolio/Getty Images; pp. 47, 67 Hulton Archive /Getty Images; p. 50 Bettmann/Getty Images; p. 54 ullstein bild /Getty Images; p. 56 Universal History Archive/Universal Images Group/Getty Images; pp. 62–63 Interim Archives/Archive Photos /Getty Images; p. 70 Win McNamee/Getty Images; p. 78 NASA /Paul E. Alers; p. 83 Science & Society Picture Library/Getty Images; p. 86 Private Collection/Bridgeman Images; p. 92 Donaldson Collection/Michael Ochs Archives/Getty Images; p. 95 Lee Young Ho /Sipa USA/Newscom; background texture Abstractor/Shutterstock.com; cover and interior pages (gold) R-studio/Shutterstock.com.

Design and Layout: Nicole Russo-Duca; Photo Researcher: Nicole DiMella